A Much-Praised Book

"So informative and fun! It brought my thought of "my time" into such a different perspective. My reality of time management was, I'm sure like most others, that I never seem to have enough. With the help from this book I can, I will and I am going to make 'my time' what I want and need."
   TABITHA RICE, CVT

"This book and the knowledge you shared is liberating, even life changing."
   JOYCE DELLAMORE, LCLT, PhCP (Netherlands)

"Dr. Pyka has written of her journey through entrepreneurship and daily life with ideas on how to solve the 'jigsaw puzzle of time', consciously investing it based on one's commitments and values. Her personable style makes this an easily accessible guide to "Time Mapping" that speaks directly to the reader."
   KENT LINDQUIST, COO

"I truly enjoyed this book. It couldn't have come at a better time for me in my mental health journey. Recently I have been working on allowing myself permission to have and do the things I want. But often feel like I am overwhelmed and don't have the "time" to do those things. As well as feel guilty for wanting to do those things for myself. Within the first few pages I found a paragraph that made things seem okay to want. "
   KELLI WILEY, CVT

"Many positive, inspirational messages!"
   DR. ADRIAN SWENSON, DC

I Can.
I Will.
I Am.

Finding the Gift of Time

Dr. Ingrid Pyka

Highlands Ranch, Colorado

Copyright © 2023 by TreeMark Publishing

First Edition

All rights reserved. No part of this publication may be reproduced, distributed, or transmitted in any form or by any means, including photocopying, recording, or other electronic or mechanical methods, without the prior written permission of the publisher.

Printed in the United States of America

I Can. I Will. I Am. Finding the Gift of Time

Pyka, Dr. Ingrid
ISBN: 978-1-948504-07-2
LCCN: 2021901782

Illustrations by Martin Pyka and Linda M. Pilgrim
Author photos by Jade Alexander
Editing by Jules Marie, 33Words Editing
Design by Bob Schram, Bookends Design

TreeMark Publishing—A Division of IBP Consulting Services LLC
9249 S. Broadway #200-830 Highlands Ranch, CO 80129, USA

www.treemarkpublishing.com

Dedicated

to Bill Carder, a friend, a teacher, a special soul forever,

and

*to Gary Barnes, a man who brings out the best
in everyone just by being the incredible person he is.*

Thank you both for making my life better.

Table of Contents

Introduction ix

CHAPTER 1 Understanding Needs and Wants.........................1

CHAPTER 2 The Why and What Game:
Learning How to Prioritize 21

CHAPTER 3 The Theory of Relativity:
Fact or Fiction? 37

CHAPTER 4 Beat the Clock, Part One:
Stop, Step Back, and Grow! 49

CHAPTER 5 Beat the Clock, Part Two:
Transferable vs. Timely 69

CHAPTER 6 Beat the Clock, Part Three:
Fixed vs. Flexible 77

CHAPTER 7 Building the Legend:
Your Master Map to Success 83

References 101

Acknowledgments 103

About the Author 109

Introduction

How often do we hear or say, "Where did the time go?"

It seemed like the harder I worked, the faster time flashed past me. I'd get up in the morning with a long list of goals for the day. Then, somehow, *whoosh*—it was day's end, and there I was, still frantically reviewing emails and texts, tackling the laundry pile, cleaning the kitchen—all while my racing mind juggled what I had yet to finish. Life was stressful and showed no signs of slowing down.

"Why can't I get things done on time, much less do them at all?!" This same frustration echoed in my thoughts—over and over, day after day, week after week, month after month.

I knew I needed a change. It had been five years since my transition from a veterinary doctor in small animal practice to private business consulting. Five *long* years, and I was still struggling to make ends meet, in addition to being exhausted and discouraged. Indeed, I needed a *big* change.

How much easier would my life have been if I had only known then what I know now, right? As is the case with so many start-up businesses, I had tackled my entrepreneurial path naïvely. Sure, as someone with a great love for research, systems, and strategies, I *thought* I was doing my part in designing a smart business plan. I understood my trade, I knew how to create effective systems and revenue sources. In reality, however, the higher my expectations were for my business, the more hats I was inadvertently forcing myself to wear—and they were heavy hats indeed! I wanted my business to grow, I was eager to provide ever-better services, as well as to handle increasingly complex administrative tasks. It was my intention to manage my entire business myself. "I can do this better than anyone else," or "It costs too much to hire someone," I kept telling myself. But with the continuously growing pressures I was facing, both in my business and in my family life, wearing so many rapidly multiplying hats was proving exceedingly difficult.

I found myself squeezing more work into what seemed like smaller time frames. Hunching over my computer, I drudged late into the night and through the weekends. Soon, I began arriving late to appointments and, horrifyingly, even forgetting a few! My follow-ups with potential clients had dropped, well, abysmally. Sleep was scarce, mistakes were rising, and opportunities that I should have been welcoming into my business and personal life were slipping away. Most importantly, I realized that I was losing the most precious asset of all: time with my two young but very quickly growing daughters. Yes, my big plan for independence was collapsing like a castle under siege.

Something was amiss. Ironically, it was the iconic dream of a "better life" that had drawn me to this path of entrepreneurship in the first place. Yet, my life did not seem better at all. Does this sound familiar?

Unknowingly, I had joined the ranks of the vast majority of new business owners—high stress, low return. Most frighteningly, I became painfully aware that 70 percent of new businesses fold within ten years.[1] Somehow, I was relieved to find that through stubborn perseverance and, at times, blind luck, I had at least made it to the halfway mark. I was determined not to add to the dismal statistic of failed businesses. But how?

I knew enough to understand that "success" was far more than "it takes money to make money." After all, my business had already managed to stay afloat without requiring significant monetary infusions. There had to be something bigger than the financial factor. Finally, I realized what "it" was. *It* was the place I struggled the most and was my most valuable investment of all: my *time*.

Boom! My world as I had known it burst open. I had struck gold.

I embraced this new principle. It was not how *hard* I worked (or played); rather, it was *how* I worked (and played). Success, growth, and satisfaction with life were better suited with how I applied, maximized, and most importantly, lived my time. At first, it was awkward to analyze my own behaviors and strategies, but soon it became a habit. I made myself acutely aware of what tasks I spent my time on, how long each took, and why I was dedicating that time to them. Then, I took it a step further. I thought about how I had been organizing my days. By reprioritizing my to-do list, and balancing *work* time, *family* time, and *free* time, I learned to define my return on investment (ROI) before, during, after, and between *moments*. That is, I applied the ROI principle not only to my financial expenditures and gains but also, as was becoming more evident, to how I spent my *time* with my family and with myself. Correction: My time was not "spent." Rather, it was about how I was *investing* my time. If I didn't get things done, it was not because I lost time but because I misappropriated the nonrenewable asset of time. In other words, I had unwisely invested in the time that was available to me.

Now things were turning around. By "things," I mean my entire view of my world was changing! Inspiration became motivation, and motivation drove action. My path was set. Finally, I absolutely knew I would succeed. I fully believed I could be that person I wanted to be! Success was mine for the taking, and I definitely took it.

I believe most of us have the best intentions when we start out. But so often we wander away from the originally planned path and allow whatever we encounter to distract us until we drift haphazardly through the swift-moving current of time. Dare we swim against the tide, we find ourselves exhausted, confused, and clambering at the shores of totally uncharted territory. Before long, we are thoroughly lost, searching desperately for a new pathway to get us back on track.

By nature, I am an organizer. Organizers like things sorted and, in their place, to achieve the best outcome. We believe progress is faster with detailed configurations, and we find reassurance through what we deem as controllable and knowing what to expect. In contrast, individuals relying on flexibility and randomness may use creativity as their foundation for innovation and success. Whether you're an organizer or a creator, or a combination, both approaches have the potential to yield remarkable results. What if we could marry these two contrasting mindsets, of strict analytics with free-flowing innovation, into an effective system that promises to deliver exactly the lifestyle we want? *This* approach would be the source of enduring success!

Through the morning musings of my journaling (which I encourage you to adopt into your routine as well), I was progressively able to put my thoughts together and develop clearer pathways for myself. My ideas began to untangle and formed into an easy and *viable* system. This technique became the blueprint for how I managed my time. The more I applied this blueprint, the more I began seeing the results of my efforts. And the more I saw the results of my now *not*-so-hard, more *effective* work, the more excited I was to tackle my upcoming tasks. Ultimately, my appreciation of this new mindset has since morphed into an intense desire to fully experience my world. This book is built upon the very essence of this experience.

Please note, by "experience" I am not referring to the number of years or practice it takes to develop a skill. *Experience* in this case is the reinvigoration of *living* life to its fullest. Experiencing the delicious smell of fresh rain. Experiencing the feel of just-washed sheets. Experiencing the joy of work. Experiencing the smile of a child skipping into the room.

Welcome to the birth of what I started calling Time Mapping—a simplified way to sort tasks, track goals, and keep priorities straight. To my surprise, in addition to reinforcing a productive schedule, the system also delivered a newfound sense of freedom. Instead of the restrictions we may typically associate with adhering to a calendar, Time Mapping served as a reassuring guide into the miracles of spontaneity. The heaviness and guilt I had felt in the past disappeared!

As I dove into the concept of Time Mapping, I discovered distinct trends in how I had made work (and life) harder for myself and I vowed to discard them. I also learned what brought me closer to finally achieving the lifestyle and success I had previously only dreamed of.

Jubilant over how Time Mapping was helping me, I started teaching these time-saving, productive methods to my clients and to any audience I could get in front of. I was met with incredible positivity and enthusiasm by analytical and creative people alike. The more I conveyed my findings, the stronger my clients and friends began experiencing the same wonderful results I had. It was as though I had found the everlasting Fountain of Youth and could share it with the world!

I Can. I Will. I Am: Finding the Gift of Time is here to put you back in the driver's seat of your day, your week, your year … your life. This book is a treasure map for you to follow: An atlas to find and capture the pot of gold at the end of the rainbow of success that may be eluding you. We cannot change our past. The future will always hide from us. What then is left for us to have and to hold? Our *now*.

Welcome! As you delve into these pages, I invite you to participate fully with an open mind and the recognition that Time Mapping allows you to journey with the perfect work-life balance you've been looking for—and that you deserve!

Ingrid

CHAPTER 1

Understanding Needs and Wants

Let us open with this: What do you want?

Society tends to dismiss this very question, often shaming "Wants" as "selfish" or "greedy." I invite you to cast that belief aside. Whether we work for our own specific prize or it is given to us as a gift, by not having our eye on the trophy in the first place, we can deny ourselves the ultimate triumph of achievement. Wanting is a good thing. It is a motivator and establishes the reward. So, to start, let's delve into rekindling a healthy dose of Wants!

I believe that most of us would generally agree that a Want is something we'd *like* to have and a Need is something we *must* have. Taking this a step further: A Need invokes negative results or implications if the Need is not gained or if it is lost. A Want, on the other hand, may suggest a powerful desire or choice, though it is not essential for survival. To be clear, "survival" in this context refers to both our biological viability (staying alive) and our ability to ultimately reach a goal or the realization of a vision.

Using these definitions as our foundation, we now face more serious questions: Are Needs or Wants more powerful in delivering us toward greater success? How does a Need influence an outcome versus a Want? Which propels us more through the steps that ultimately lead to achieving satisfaction: (a) the systems and logic as the driving forces of a Need or (b) the emotional, deep-rooted intensity of a Want?

I realize that this may appear to be diving into a philosophical reflection. Stay with me. For effective Time Mapping, it is vital to understand this dichotomy. Why? Because the very essence of *what* you do *when* is driven purely by your commitment level. Hence, is it the Need or the Want that becomes the motivator? How dedicated you are to a particular outcome predicts the likelihood of the intended result coming to fruition. What happens when you Need something? No questions asked, no excuses made, regardless of the challenges—the fact is that as long as it is theoretically possible you somehow attain this Need. In contrast, there must be enough passion (emotion) behind a Want before no obstacle is deemed too large to stand in the way of the goal. Otherwise, interest wanes; energy, effort, and ensuing actions dwindle to nothing. The result? The Want (goal) fades away, never to be obtained.

My father always impressed me with his diligence and commitment to work. He showed me how survival can mean so much more than staying alive. He approached everything wholeheartedly and never stopped learning or applying new ideas with his constant drive to improve professionally and personally. I saw him expand his career as he poked through a napkin with a scope to perform "surgery" on an orange on the dining room table. This primed him to become one of the first orthopedists to adopt arthroscopy, a now commonplace, less-invasive joint surgery with much faster and easier recovery. I watched him evenings and weekends relentlessly tackle the most difficult Bach or Beethoven compositions to satisfy his incredible passion for the piano. And I learned the power of persistence through the stories he shared from the trenches.

As a teenager, my father was torn from his studies as a career pianist in a prestigious music conservatory to serve in World War II. His experience as a soldier is an incredible story for another time. He escaped injury, never hurt anyone (unwittingly even saved the life of an "enemy") and, by determining what he needed to do to survive, did exactly that – he stayed alive.

After the war, he returned home to find his community all but destroyed, with most of his family dead or missing. Despite his despair, my father worked nights, enrolled in a university medical program by day, and spent whatever precious "spare" time he had in his tiny, rented room, diligently studying. He had no comforts and barely was able to feed himself. Again, he survived. Nine years later, he offered his lovely bride and newborn son a once-in-a-lifetime opportunity to start fresh, away from a country still stricken by the devastations of war. Soon, the *USS General W.C. Langfitt* carried his young family to the land of opportunity—the United States of America. Their meager possessions included one trunk and two suitcases – it was all they needed to begin the new life they dreamt of. Between the nasty waves of seasickness, my ever-practical Papi even earned a few extra dollars shoveling coal into the steam engine to fuel the eleven-day voyage across the stormy Atlantic Ocean. When they arrived, my father knew only basic English (which he had taught himself), and at that time, my mother spoke only German. They quickly discovered that most of what was in the trunk was destroyed—shattered during transport. Regardless, survival once more prevailed. Once settled in America, the family grew by two more boys and myself and finally, my brave father could do more than survive—he flourished.

I struggled to understand the resilience he had shown in the face of the horrendous conditions and circumstances he encountered. I felt paralyzed with fear just picturing those struggles.

"Papi," I asked, "how did you do it? How did you live through such appalling circumstances and those awful times?"

He looked at me and matter-of-factly responded, "Simple. That's just how it was and you did what you *needed* to do."

I still believe my father as one of the wisest men that lived. To his point, when we Want (desire) something enough, we figure out what we Need to do to get it.

Emotion drives commitment. And, when we *believe* we absolutely Need something (regardless whether we actually do), that dominant sense of your ultimate and present-tense *I Am* surpasses everything else that may stand in your way. Consider the astounding strength harnessed when a random bystander lifts a car by themselves because the Need to save the person trapped beneath just "makes it happen." Or when a mother rushes into a burning building to save her child. Running past flames choked by heavy smoke is likely far from something she would ever Want to do. My father always said that he did what he Needed to do to get food into his belly. Such Needs are propelled by far greater powers than the risks faced. The energy of this inner Need is the prevailing force that inspires us and moves us past any obstacle that may stand in our way.

Let's apply this Need versus Want concept to some instances we may find in a business setting. Imagine that after years of wooing a large company, you finally secure an interview with the CEO to discuss onboarding them as a client. Can we agree that having a large organization like this sign your contract is an example of an intense Want, or a desire? Let us presume it is a solid "Yes!" You Want this client very, very much. It will be your greatest opportunity and could translate into far more lucrative deals in the future. Every previous action leading up to this moment was strategically planned: contacts secured, conversations held with key department heads, collaborations organized with colleagues and significant leads. You showed up however and whenever the process commanded. Without the substantial effort put forth over the previous years, it's unlikely that you would have garnered the credibility and connections that ultimately attracted the trust and attention of this company and its CEO. You *Needed* to do everything we just listed to achieve this final decisive *Want*.

We'll add another layer to this story to further express the important nuance between Need and Want. Let's say that with all the last-minute preparations, you didn't realize until the very morning of the interview that you didn't have anything clean and pressed to wear. Obviously, an old pair of torn jeans and a faded t-shirt is unacceptable for the executive suite. You have options: speed-wash a small load, run to the dry cleaner with a rush order, race to a store to buy something new, or, yikes, perhaps even borrow from a friend. You Need to wear something professional because you Want to make a positive impression – right? Will you? Of course, you will. You will be impeccably attired. Why? Because, again, you have a Want (your appearance at your possibly once-in-a-lifetime shot) that you have ranked as a ten. This Want is your current top priority. Whatever else Needs to be done will fall into place because of your 100 percent commitment to your appearance.

To illustrate Wants further, let's modify this example to an upcoming event for Grandma's eighty-third-birthday celebration. The entire family will be there!

But, uh-oh, once more you've been so busy with work, along with a leaky pipe in the basement and grocery shopping for a sick neighbor, that you are behind on laundry and have nothing appropriate to wear. You Want to look nice for the event, but in this instance, you believe it's more important to be on time for the big shout-out of "Surprise!" when Grandma enters the room. You trust that your family will understand. They really won't care what you're wearing—they'll just be happy that you're there. Though your commitment to attend is high, getting dressed up is very low in your immediate priorities. At this point, your last clean sweatshirt is good enough! In contrast to your meeting with the CEO, where you Needed to make the best professional impression, the Need to arrive in time for the special family moment surpasses the desire to look your best.

Adjust the circumstances one last time: You've been invited to your neighbor's wedding. It's one of those evening-gown-and-black-tie, five-star exclusive events. For months you've heard about the detailed preparations for this elegant affair. Assuming the same hectic schedule has led you to neglect your clothing yet again, you are now faced with this latest last-minute scramble. Your search for the perfect (and clean) ensemble soars back up to an imperative Need because you Want to respect the formalities. In this case, your efforts to find the right attire jump back to high.

Why am I going into such detail about what to wear? These are real-life examples that most of us can relate to. By bringing these three wardrobe scenarios into full perspective, the dedication to your Needed actions with each very different setting is reflected by how much effort you actually put into the outfits. This commitment weakens or strengthens depending on the ultimate value you give each end goal. Broaden the application to any scenario you wish. By consciously determining how much you Want any vision (goal, mission, desire—whatever you choose to call it), you effectively define your own obligation to fulfill each of your actions and what you Need to do to get there—or not. Your choice.

1 Time Plot 1:
Starting with Your Want List (aka Wish List)

Let's begin with some goal-setting. This is about your desires. What do you Want in your career, lifestyle, and relationships? Where do you Want to travel? Who do you Want to meet? What do you Want to learn? What do you Want to add or change about where you live? How do you Want to spend your free time?

Write down your thoughts in the next two pages by using these three questions to guide you with your Want List:

1. What do you Want to **Have**?
2. What do you Want to **Do**?
3. What or *who* do you Want to **Be**?

Be open-minded to your "when's" as well:

- What do you Want to have **this month**?
- How do you Want to feel **this year**?
- Where do you Want to see yourself in the **next five years**?

Make a list of everything you Want and/or wish for. Explore the opportunities and play with an open mindset. Dream big and assume anything as being possible!

Wants:

More Wants:

With the list of goals (your Wants) you just created, you have gained a menu of "I Can's." You've put the initial concepts out into the universe: I Can get a new car. I Can take the vacation. I Can _____ *(insert any of your desires to complete the sentence)*.

Yet many of these statements may still feel like intangible dreams to you. So how do we get you closer to your Wants? Simple. Initiate your first transition: Exchange "I Can" with "I Will."

We equally discourage or inspire our own future with what we tell ourselves. Expressing that you'll *probably* or *maybe* attain your goal crumbles the very essence of forward movement. Pursuing a dream that you don't even believe in erodes your core foundation to success. This is why transforming your Want from a suggestion (I Can) into a concise and decisive phrase that begins with "I Will …" is so important. By having faith in your goal, you establish the critical groundwork to a path you then choose to follow. "I Will" triggers a series of believable and viable steps and sparks the strong mindset necessary for your dream to become real.

I just mentioned viable steps. The key word here is "viable." The commitment you attach to your actions is what evolves your goal from possible to probable and, ultimately, actionable. A pledge of authenticity and dedication inherently comes with declaring "I Will"—especially when spoken aloud and with conviction. Your vision begins to materialize and the domino effect takes over. As my friend, TEDx speaker and prominent business coach Gary Barnes, says, "Facts are stories until they become beliefs." I cannot reinforce this enough. True belief carries with it a gripping promise and is the powerful motivator to success. It becomes your mantra, your guiding force.

By building strong intentions and clearly validating the efforts to yourself, you naturally accept an opportunity for its true potential and beyond. You metaphorically set yourself on a mapped-out flight plan, ready to launch the goal into reality.

It is human nature to think big, and in the previous dreaming exercise I asked for really big thinking! As a result, before us now lies a looming list of bright, shiny objects, as we like to call them. But as grandiose as these goals may seem, the reality is that we can't do everything at once (much more to come on this subject!).

So how much do you Want it?

To eliminate the overwhelm and focus on what is most important to you, I would like to introduce you to the Want-o-Meter. This scale is a magical tool that allows you to bring your big wish list into reasonable perspective and to help you prioritize. When applying the Want-o-Meter to your wishes and desires, use it as a power gauge. Pretend you have your Want in hand: you are living it, breathing it, tasting it. How much satisfaction do you see with this accomplishment? What are the gains or losses after you have received or achieved your Want in contrast to what you have now? The Want-o-Meter scores value to anything you wish or desire.

2 Time Plot 2:
Applying the Want-o-Meter.

Go back to pp. 10-11 and review your Want/Wish List from Time Plot 1. In the real world, we are often working on more than one goal at a time. But this book is about simplifying life, so, for now, use your Want-o-Meter to order your Wants from 1 (I truly, truly Want) down to 10 (I Want but not as much). Consider ranking only your top three to five Wants initially and leave the rest for a secondary reevaluation in the future.

Next, we build the strategic base for your success. To start, look at your top Want and identify at least three steps you *Need* to do (must do) first to achieve this Want. For example, to play a real game of basketball, you need five players, a ball and a hoop. Or, for a new brand, you need the logo image, colors and font. Think it through. If you feel overwhelmed, you don't have to hit the moon with the first launch: Small steps can be just as powerful, sometimes even more so. Take a deep breath … in … out … in … out … allow yourself to relax. What could bring you even the tiniest bit closer to your #1 Want?

3a Time Plot 3a:
Transforming the Want into a Strategic Foundation

Combine your Want with its Needs into the following framework:

I Want to _____

My first three Needs to get closer or to achieve my Want are:

1. _____

2. _____

3. _____

3b Time Plot 3b: Solidifying the Mindset

Insert your Want in the first blank, and rewrite the above steps from 3a into the following statement:

In order to _____,

I Need to _____,

_____,

and _____.

What a valuable plan you have just created as your foundation! You have clearly defined and prioritized your desires, and you now have the treasure map, or at least the beginnings of one, for how to get there!

Perhaps you were fortunate—meaning the simplified process you just followed was enough to lead you straight to your final goal. Maybe you Needed less than three steps, or, if more were necessary, you were still easily able to list them. More likely than not, however, at least some of your steps (Needs) are incomplete or may feel too daunting for you to accomplish at this time. The solution? Make them reasonable and achievable by repeating what we just did in Time Plot 3 and position the Need you can't complete yet into a new Want. Then establish another set of Need-to steps to accomplish this latter Want (goal). If you don't know four other basketball players, how about reaching out to a couple of your friends that you know would like to play? You can build the rest of the team with people *they* know. If you don't know which colors are best for your logo, then you may "Need" someone to help you. Begin with a search for graphic designers or by asking your friends or colleagues for referrals. These redefined action steps become your new Needs.

Example:

1. To make the perfect cup of coffee (the Want), I Need one cup of water, two teaspoons of ground coffee beans, water, and a coffeemaker.

2. But, alas, I go into the kitchen and realize I have no coffee.
   a. Shift the Need: In order to get more coffee beans (my new Want),
   b. I Need to get my wallet, drive to the grocery store, and buy a new bag.
      - Doggone it! I encounter another obstacle: I don't have enough gas in my car to get to the market.
      - New Want = Fill the gas tank at the nearest gas station.

As you move through each Want and subsets of Needs, ultimately, you'll be seated peacefully at your dining table enjoying a steaming cup of fresh, home-brewed, delicious coffee.

Strengthening what you *can* do into something you *will* do is about breaking down your obstacles into smaller, more concrete, and attainable action steps. Keep cycling through "This is what I Want" and "What do I Need to do to get it?" until you accomplish the original goal you established in Time Plot 1.

But how do you know what to do first when you are juggling multiple tasks (or Needs and Wants) at once? Read on.

> **NOTE:** *The words "Need" and "Want" have been capitalized in this chapter to accentuate and differentiate each. For the remainder of this book, unless specifically referring to the Needs/Wants of this chapter, we will not be capitalizing these terms.*

CHAPTER 2

The Why and What Game: Learning How to Prioritize

As I pursued how to maximize my productivity and efficiency, I recognized I had to understand time at a much deeper level. Books were fascinating but did not fully satisfy the questions I had of what time really meant and how it related to my career *and* personal life. Where should I go from here? My grandmother's words came to the rescue.

Oma (as everyone called her—family or not) was the little, old lady who welcomed the neighborhood kids for a visit. And visit they did! They knew she would always have a smile for them. She never scolded and eagerly listened to all of their adventures (many made-up—but she never let on she knew that) and, usually had a tasty chocolate bar to console the owner of the skinned knee who appeared at her door. Adults found themselves attracted to her warmth and obvious compassion too—even if they didn't know her. With a merry laugh none could resist, Oma was a four-foot-something contagious ball of energy. My grandmother was loved by everyone who met her and I will always cherish the time I had with her.

Yet, decades after her passing, I found myself wondering, why did she still *inspire* me? It was then that the meaning of a story she had shared with me long ago fully sunk in:

"I remember when I was just barely in my teens," she began, "there was this absolutely beautiful girl in my class. I envied how pretty she was and always wished I was more like her. Then one day when she came to class, I noticed something peculiar and peered closer. Oh, my! The telltale signs of a bath not gone well!"

I should explain a bit of my grandmother's past here. Oma was born at the turn of the nineteenth century. Roads were still dirt with foot traffic, horses, and buggies relentlessly stirring up the dust. Pedestrian-power was how most people, including my grandmother and her friends, got around.

Back to the young lady of my grandmother's envy. Oma continued, giggling.

"Indeed, her lovely face was freshly washed, but, she had not bothered to go any further! Her neck! Unbeknownst to the poor girl, a thick layer of grimy dust coated her neck, contrasting grotesquely to her fair face. To make things worse," Oma gestured up and down her own throat with her pinky finger, "We could see tracks of clean skin where the rivulets of water had trickled down her neck. She looked worse than had she not washed at all!"

There was a special closeness with my grandmother as we chuckled in this complete girlish moment. My grandmother watched me as I relished the grooming *faux-pas* of a young schoolgirl from so many decades ago. Then Oma shared the real purpose behind her story:

"Always be watching others, *mein Liebchen*. When you find yourself admiring someone, whether it's how they carry themselves, how they help others, what they're saying, what they're wearing, what they're doing, then do it too. Copy them! Learn from others.

"But, if you *don't* like what they are doing," she continued, "then don't do it yourself! I can tell you that I always made sure I thoroughly scrubbed my face and neck from then on! At least to my collar!" she added mischievously and peeled off into gales of sweet laughter.

I now understand that the time she spent with others had been far more wisely invested than I ever realized. She was constantly observing and learning. Now it was time for me to dive deep into the wealth of knowledge far beyond classroom lessons and books. I appreciated that paying attention to those around me was the key to my time dilemma—What stories do they have to tell?

So, in 2016, I began interviewing individuals of a variety of ages, demographics, cultures, ethnicities, socioeconomic backgrounds, and more. I held in-person conversations, created online polls and surveys in my quest for answers. I received an astonishing influx of responses and was delighted to discover distinctive trends in how people perceive time.

My research was straightforward: I created a survey comprising three open-ended questions, with the exact phrasing that follows and in the same sequence:

1. *"What does time mean to you?"*
2. *"What do you see being the two most frustrating things about not having enough time?"*
3. *"What is one word that describes having the right amount of time for everything you want to do?"*

I interviewed hundreds of people, and I am excited to reveal the results of my discovery about time. Over the next pages, I will share how to embrace these valuable insights and how they apply to the overall positive Time Mapping experience. Customizing needs and desires allows you to not only prioritize but also to forgive certain facets of your life. The purpose of Time Mapping is to lose the guilt, decrease stress, and ultimately, achieve more with less time than you ever thought possible. You get to discover how best to relate these concepts of time to your own world and welcome extraordinary results with a resounding and proud appreciation of "I Am!"

My first survey question:
"What does time mean to you?"

After interviewees overcame their initial perplexity about such an esoteric topic, they quickly transformed into philosophical and introspective "experts." I asked for only a sentence or two, but within moments a floodgate of opinions would burst open, and I could hardly close them!

Here is an example:

"Feelings mark time better than clocks, watches, and calendars," wrote Alex in her fascinating and unsolicited 522-word reply!

Originally, I had anticipated that most responses would allude to the materialism of clocks and calendars. After all, humanity has been tracking time with measurement tools since the Bronze Age. But I was quite mistaken, as fewer than a handful of responders even referenced measurable increments, such as minutes or days. The few who did immediately pointed out that these markers were merely "mankind's invention."

People spoke with much deeper language as they correlated their experiences to the meaning of Time:

- "Memories."
- "Aging."
- "Valuable commodity."
- "Luxury, burden, challenge."
- "A tool for balance and success."

To some, time seems to be a constant, while for others it represents shifting values that continually cycle throughout their lives. Several people remarked that time means appreciation or prioritization.

Time has been associated with limitations, and suggested as a treasure that could be given as well as received, but never bought or sold. Time has been translated as abilities, potential, not having enough, wishes, a nonrenewable resource. Some respondents were emphatic about time meaning something only *they* could control themselves, while on the opposite end of the spectrum, there were those admitting defeat to any sort of "time management."

The list of what purpose time holds in our existence seems endless. What does this all mean?

Imagine a bucket of water. As it stands, this water means nothing to you. But when you need it, want it, use it, or it impacts or touches you in some way, its purpose changes. You can drink it to quench your thirst, or frantically pitch it aside to save your sinking boat. Or perhaps it is just one of the millions of gallons of water holding your ship afloat as you sail across the ocean's rippling reflections during a warm summer sunset. It is all just water, H_2O, its significance to you soley dependent on its use by, or impact on, you. Water does not care what you do with it. Time is the same way. Time does not care.

I repeat: *Time does not care*. Like the bucket of water, it simply exists. You can, however, give *your* time value, worth, and meaning when you *pay attention* to what you are doing with it.

Collectively, interviewees seemed to agree that the *meaning* of time had nothing to do with where or how we spend our lives. Rather, it is the *value* of what we are doing in the *where* and *how* we spend our lives. And thus, encapsulating the many responses:

<blockquote>Time means value.</blockquote>

Reconsider the Wants you defined in chapter one's Time Plot 1 (pp. 10-11). Remember the Want-o-Meter? As you assigned values to each Want, you saw your priorities naturally sort themselves in the order most effective or desirable to you.

It is important to recognize that each of these rankings may vary based on the circumstances in our lives and their influences on us here and now versus there and later. Some may be strong, short-term aspirations, while others may not realize their full potential for years to come. We must also keep in mind the myriad categories, ranging from financial health, special relationships, resilient self-care, and so much more. How each person determines priorities is an entirely individualized interpretation and may shift throughout the many, many, *many* stages of life. This is normal!

The likelihood that each Want comes to fruition (or not) is directly related to your commitment—the value you assigned to it. Why? Because you just set your *commitment* level to each of the follow-through *actions* needed. If the result is not that important to you, you likely will not get it done. If it is high-ranking, then, as we demonstrated in chapter one, you will, however humanly possible, tackle each of those action steps. If you don't know how, you have just pledged yourself to figure it out. This is so critical to time management that I must reiterate: Your Wants are defined by the value you give each.

I invite you to periodically review the ranking of your Wants from Time Plot 1 to help you gauge the significance of each Want during that period in your life. As you reach the end of your perhaps long list, some Wants may even fall away from time to time. As a result, it will become easy for you to let go of the many guilt-free stressors in your life simply because you consciously realized they were no longer important to you. They have fallen off the Want-o-Meter. It's like clearing your plate of cold or tasteless leftovers to make room for your favorite fresh pizza or a new mouth-watering dessert.

But do as we may, the reality is that we still face extraordinary pressures when, inevitably, too many "top" priorities present themselves at the same time. I know I often felt this time-squeeze before I understood Time Mapping. To better grasp this overwhelm, I carefully chose this next question for my survey:

"What do you see being most frustrating about not having enough time?"

At this point, I would imagine that many of you would reply: "Not getting things done!" Indeed, that was exactly what I said! So, instead, I revised the question:

"What do you see being the two most frustrating things about not having enough time?"

Now we are forced to face the limitations bestowed upon us by our mere twenty-four-hour days.

- "I want to, but I can't."
- "Missed opportunities."
- "Unsustainable."
- "Too old."

Wait, didn't we just declare that time holds so much value? Yet here we see a strong force working *against* this very conclusion! Oh, the aggravation we feel when there is not enough time with lovers, children, friends, hobbies, vacations, sleeping, and more!

Are you surprised, then, that I have found that many people quite readily blame themselves? Recent college graduate Chris quickly admitted:

"I know that [the frustration I feel with not having enough time] is probably my own fault."

Add to that, responses like these:

"Not able to appreciate the moment."
"Giving in to distractions."
"I'm left with a feeling that I need to be more efficient."
"I don't do enough things that make me happy."

Do these sentiments sound familiar? What does this negativity do to our daily lives?

Picture the familiar half-empty or half-full glass conundrum. Let us approach this from an entirely different perspective. You see, the real question should be: Why does full or empty even matter?

Let's return to the example of the bucket of water. In this case, rather than the existence of the water, the attention focuses on the *amount* of water. And what is the relevance of that quantity to its own existence or presence? Irrelevant. It just *is*. It is not about how much water there is; rather it is about what you do with the remaining supply that matters. To help you appreciate this more, imagine your favorite beverage in the glass. Close your eyes. What if you just choose to drink what's there and savor the flavor and everything that comes with it?

We all have the same twenty-four hours in a day, and as we instinctively know, we cannot be in two places at once. But we sure make every effort to, don't we? Because of this, so often we anguish about whether to turn left or right. Do we stop to pick up some bagels for the study group, or arrive early to finish a report? Do I call the friend I haven't spoken to in months, do I veg out on the couch, or catch a much-needed nap?

Yet when a deadline draws near, somehow, right or wrong, we always do *something*. You are on a basketball court and the point guard throws you the ball. Regardless of your athletic abilities, you won't intentionally stand there and wait until the ball smacks you in the face. Either you jump aside to dodge it, whip up your hands to catch it, or at least knock it to the side. Why? Because in the seconds it takes to assess your circumstances ("Uh-oh, the ball is approaching my head"), you have an innate capacity to wade through all the options available and ultimately choose which action to take. The action is a choice based on the value to your circumstance (avoiding a ball to the nose or the ability to shoot for the basket). Presuming you have enough time to react before the ball reaches you, you *do* either step to the side or prepare to catch it.

Though it may be frustrating to seemingly "not have enough time to do what you want" (i.e., the basketball crashes into your face), it is important to realize that it is not about whether there is or is not enough time. It is clearly about the ability to access the time you have and apply it to what you decide is most valuable to you. How you access your time is not about the past or the future. Through conscious awareness, you get to make choices to the best of your ability, based on what you have, feel, and see with what you know and experience *now*.

Wherever you are, whatever you do, permit yourself to choose what brings the highest value to the moment. It is important to acknowledge that this means you must also get comfortable with what you let go of. Satisfaction with life comes down to no regrets for what you choose to do as well as no regrets for what you choose *not* to do. Seize the ball, and even if you must pick it up from where it landed, score a 3-pointer!

I then asked my final question:

"What is one word that describes having the right amount of time for everything you want to do?"

When I carefully developed this question for the study, I expected the majority of participants to offer patronizing replies like "utopia" or "impossible." Once again, I was proven quite wrong.

Instead, faces suddenly smiled. I saw wishful thinking, sensed relief, and found myself listening to overwhelmingly uplifting sentiments. Behold the top responses:

- "Balance."
- "Peace."
- "Happiness."

Many more similar answers echoed over and over in my rapidly building database: "Calm." "Love." "Relief." "Ecstatic!"

The answers to this last question made me realize that these positive and enriching interpretations are the core of a powerful belief system. Ultimately, experiencing the "right amount of time" is not about waiting for a cause and effect, but instead believing in and *living* your personal reward now.

If you have not already done so, I challenge you to ask yourself the same three questions about time. Review your reactions and recognize the integral relationships among (1) knowing what you Want, (2) embracing what you Need to do to obtain it, and (3) accepting that the **value**, the **choice**, and the **belief** in how you have invested the moment is right for you.

1. *"What does time mean to you?"*
2. *"What two things do you see being most frustrating about not having enough time?"*
3. *"What is one word that describes having the right amount of time for everything you want to do?"*

Long ago my high school counselor Mr. Henry shared with me some of the most precious words of truth I now live by. We were sitting in his tiny office. His enormous presence, with his belly seeming as wide as he was tall, could not be ignored. I slouched on the wooden stool as thousands of other confused seniors had likely done before me. At the time, I was faced with choosing between two incredible opportunities for college and didn't know which to pick. Wasn't this decision going to determine the rest of my life? The deadline was looming. I had to decide. Agonizing and desperate, I was in tears hoping that my trusted adviser would give me an easy answer.

He leaned forward on the squeaky, sagging desk chair that had seen much better days. His normally jolly eyes turned serious:

"No matter which path you choose, Ingrid, be happy with it. Never look back and wish to have made the other decision."

How right Mr. Henry was. I would not be the person I am today without my now-alma mater Colorado State University in Fort Collins. Whether I liked them or not, the twists and turns that lead me to here, also gifted me with two amazing daughters and a host of wonderful friends and colleagues. I am better because of the lessons I have learned and through the experiences I have gained on this journey. I have embraced the achievements created through my own choices even when it felt like some of the decisions were made for me. It was *I* who choreographed my dance of life with each step, each moment standing brightly before the next.

Accept the power you held within yourself that led you to the choices you made in the past. "If I had known then what I know now" is a lie. You did *not* know then what you know now, and you will *never* know then what you learned even split seconds later. Why you responded the way you did was because of what was going on *then*. The reality is that if you were in the same situation again, within the same context of what you knew, felt, heard, and experienced at that time, you would default to the same decision again. This is why you made that choice in the first place—the correct choice for you.

"I Am Who I Am Because I Am."

So, rest at ease. Remember, if you want something that you believe would have come from having taken an alternate path in the past, you can still create a new strategy designed to lead you to that destination again—with the added power of what you do know now.

4 Time Plot 4:
Releasing the Guilt

Return to your application of the Want-o-Meter in Time Plot's 3a and 3b (pp.16-17). I am going to challenge you here. You may experience strong emotions as you journal through this next phase and that's okay. Consider some of the challenges you will face and fears you may have churning inside you as you take the steps to fulfill your dreams. What must you let go of to reach the goal?

What is the Need? What will you have to do or not do to accomplish it?

CHAPTER 3

The Theory of Relativity: Fact or Fiction?

How time relates to your life is dependent on one factor—you. Not time management, not anyone else, just you.

Thirty-five hundred years ago, Egyptians were credited with being the first to split the day/night cycle into "hourly" segments. To further develop timekeeping, the Babylonians and Greeks studied the cyclic patterns of the sun, stars, and moon that created a twenty-four-hour day. There were alternative proposals to divide the day, such as the decimal-based French Revolutionary Time, a short-lived model of a ten-hour day. It officially launched in France in 1793, but only lasted as the country's standard for less than two years.[2] Ultimately, the world settled on the twenty-four-hour day, divided into two twelve-hour cycles, with sixty minutes per hour and sixty seconds per minute, that we follow today.

Going beyond this brief history lesson, it is important to realize that no matter how we shuffle our blocks of time, a day is just that: one day. There are twenty-four finite hours in our daylight and night time. Even if we were using another clock or calendar design, one day *is and always will be* the time it takes for the earth to revolve around itself. We can never push more "time" into our day beyond those hours, minutes, and *moments* that form each day/night cycle.

Stay with me as I introduce one more slightly technical concept. Shortly, we will simplify and tie each of these elements into an easy and practical application.

The Pauli exclusion principle states that no two objects can occupy the same space at one time.[3] The gigantic formulas and physics lessons to prove it notwithstanding, we can accept this premise because we have experienced it firsthand. When we swing a bat, the ball doesn't dissipate through the wood (or aluminum). Picture the infamous cat napping on top of a computer keyboard. Perhaps a sweet sight, but for the hapless writer wanting to finish a paragraph, it's a bit more frustrating. There is no way to type *through* the body of fluff. Or, go to the household junk drawer. As long as the roll of packing tape doesn't lay flat in the drawer, it will never completely shut—no matter how desperately we shove it closed.

When my daughters were young, they had a small wooden box with a sliding lid to seal the contents. Within the container, there were fifteen building blocks of various shapes and sizes. Taking them out, my girls could play and build however their dexterity and creativity inspired them. When arranged in a specific configuration, the red, blue, and yellow figures fit perfectly back in the box. *Swoosh*, the top slipped back into place for neat, tidy storage.

Now let's translate this principle to the concept of time. Shift your perspective just a bit and designate one time period as one of these tangible, three-dimensional blocks from our toy box. Pretend the entire container represents one moment (whatever that may be—a minute, an hour, a day). Applying Pauli's rule to the blocks, no two can rest in the same place at the same time. The triangular wedge in the middle row cannot take the place of the cube on the bottom because (a) the space for the triangle is a different shape and (b) we would have nowhere else to fit the cube. Each of the fifteen pieces has its own unique spot creating a neat, whole package, like jigsaw pieces completing a puzzle. Again, no two things can be in the same space at the same time.

Relating the analogy of a wooden block equaling time used in scheduling, each block symbolizes an appointment or task in your day: the triangle for a haircut, the square for shopping, one of the rectangles represents travel, another rectangle, a friendly game of soccer. The box is the container of our twenty-four-hour day. Just as the blocks cannot be in the same place at the same time, you cannot be bowling while grocery shopping! It is impossible for you to sit on a flight to Chicago for a business meeting while cheering on your favorite soccer team from the stands. And, as much as we joke about it, we all know that box of time refuses to expand for the twenty-*fifth* hour, no matter how hard we stretch or push.

Let us not confuse exclusivity with multitasking. Could you be getting a haircut in the bleachers while cheering on the goalie? A bit odd, but I'm sure it could be arranged! Indeed, there are times when we "multitask," but we must ask ourselves, "What is the value of that time spent when we're not entirely focused on the task?" (Dare I mention the countless hours stolen by ever-present mobile devices, distracting us at nearly every moment? Ah, well, I'll reserve that for another book.) Indeed, by nature, we do multiple tasks concurrently. We may be on a conference call while we peruse our emails. Perhaps we listen to an audiobook while folding the laundry. But mentally, are we focusing on the right things at the same time? Truly focused? One hundred percent? You do laundry with an audiobook in the background. You pick up a sock and look for the match. As you search for the other green sock, did you hear and understand what the detective just asked the witness in the past few minutes of the narration? You're driving home from work, replaying in your mind a conversation with a coworker earlier in the day. How many times have you or have you heard someone sheepishly admit to driving past the intended exit because you/they weren't paying attention —aka, "deep in thought?"

The reality is that it is impossible to multitask and focus on each task successfully. The human brain cannot process two things at the same time. Imagine a yellow ball. Now visualize a purple grape. Notice how the first object vanished as soon as you went to the next one.

Let's return to the box of blocks. Pretend there is now a container that holds a total of twenty-four equally sized blocks—two layers tall, three rows of four. Each unit (block) represents one hour and all twenty-four blocks collectively represent one day. Remove one block and chop it into smaller blocks to indicate minutes and reinsert the set into the same spot. Or envision a box of seven larger blocks to represent one week or even thirty smaller units as the month of June. It all still fits in the box. Regardless of how you divide, subdivide, or stack the blocks back together, the *container* symbolizing the specific period of time must remain its same size. A week is a week, a day is a day, right? Fact: We cannot stretch or reduce the days. Though we can subdivide and clump the periods, time as a whole is not elastic.

Though we have established that we can't effectively superimpose one unit on top of another (multitasking), we *can* adjust the size (number of moments = minutes, days, etc.) per action, and also nothing is keeping us from rearranging them (now versus later). We *can* control the cube sizes and quantities (tasks and time frames allotted to each) in a manner to still fit within the container. Perhaps move the haircut (two fifteen-minute blocks) *before* the game (six fifteen-minute blocks). Switch your flight to nonstop (three one-hour units) so you arrive home one hour earlier with time to pick up dinner (one half-hour unit). Imagine having an additional thirty minutes of family time before the day is done! Section or fashion your day as works best for you as long as all the blocks fit into the imaginary (but also real) constraints of a twenty-four-hour day. This is how to successfully use Time Mapping principles.

Use *value-choice-belief* as your compass. Then establish your level of commitment to each block's size, location (where it is in your schedule), and to the action itself. These commitments drive your intended time management strategy.

In Time Mapping, I encourage users to create time allotments for every activity of each day. Acknowledge dedicated time for family, work, friends, holidays, events, free time, and yes, even sleeping. Some days you may have to work late; others might allow more flexibility. The intention is not to force you to be a constant slave to your calendar. Far from it. Rather, consciously and visually acknowledging these elements in your life will yield a positive anchor. Time Mapping your blocks serves as a reminder. You will become fully aware of your commitments to work, others, and yourself, similarly learning what you can also release.

I mentioned sleep in the previous paragraph. What *about* sleeping? Rest may sound trivial to some of you, but you must account for the minimum hours you need for shut-eye. In our chaotic, overachieving culture, we've seen a decline in sleep time. Are you experiencing this too? Studies continue to show the many benefits our bodies and minds gain from getting a good night's sleep. So schedule sleep! You'll feel refreshed and be more effective at work. Your creativity will blossom and your life satisfaction levels will jump exponentially. The same applies to exercise and nutrition. Reserve blocks in your schedule to take care of yourself.

Do you feel confined by only having twenty-four hours in a day? I admit that I do. But I found the solution: The half-empty/half-full glass of water mentioned in chapter two. Expand your mindset and break free from self-imposed restrictions. Remember, it isn't about how *much* time we have; it's about how we "invest" our time. Fill each moment with appreciation and savor what you have! As Ralph Waldo Emerson said, "It's about the journey, not the destination."

Time Mapping is the art of creating and arranging your blocks to best fit in your container. As soon as I confidently embraced the Time Mapping technique, I accomplished my goals more quickly and effectively than I had in the past. By establishing fluid Time Mapping, that is, a schedule that can adjust and mold around your wants and needs, a previously fictional dream transforms into a new reality. Fact: You will respect your boundaries and, at the same time, generate more freedom in your life. Perhaps even more importantly, you can discover and maintain the work-life balance that you desire. You'll gain a sense of freedom as, by choice, you spend less time on certain activities while committing more time to others. Tiny tweaks can yield a powerful sense of calm, control, and flexibility.

Now let's take a look at Time Plot 5a and 5b as we consider exactly how we spent or invested our time during the past week.

5a Time Plot 5a: Plotting Your <u>Before</u>

	Monday	Tuesday	Wednesday
12:00 a.m.			
1:00 a.m.			
2:00 a.m.			
3:00 a.m.			
4:00 a.m.			
5:00 a.m.			
6:00 a.m.			
7:00 a.m.			
8:00 a.m.			
9:00 a.m.			
10:00 a.m.			
11:00 a.m.			
12:00 p.m.			
1:00 p.m.			
2:00 p.m.			
3:00 p.m.			
4:00 p.m.			
5:00 p.m.			
6:00 p.m.			
7:00 p.m.			
8:00 p.m.			
9:00 p.m.			
10:00 p.m.			
11:00 p.m.			

As much as possible, map out what you did during this past week.

Thursday	Friday	Saturday	Sunday

5b Time Plot 5b: Plotting Your <u>After</u>

	Monday	Tuesday	Wednesday
12:00 a.m.			
1:00 a.m.			
2:00 a.m.			
3:00 a.m.			
4:00 a.m.			
5:00 a.m.			
6:00 a.m.			
7:00 a.m.			
8:00 a.m.			
9:00 a.m.			
10:00 a.m.			
11:00 a.m.			
12:00 p.m.			
1:00 p.m.			
2:00 p.m.			
3:00 p.m.			
4:00 p.m.			
5:00 p.m.			
6:00 p.m.			
7:00 p.m.			
8:00 p.m.			
9:00 p.m.			
10:00 p.m.			
11:00 p.m.			

As much as possible, map out how you plan the upcoming week.

Thursday	Friday	Saturday	Sunday

CHAPTER 4

Beat the Clock, Part One: Stop, Step Back, and Grow!

In the previous chapters, you learned the components that make up the cycle of time. In a systematic, yet flexible manner, you can now determine what is important to you and how your actions fit within a designated day, week, month, or even year. The question still arises: How do you best align your actions to achieve your ultimate goals?

In one of my previous books—"Stop Step Back & GROW: The 3 Keys to Long-Term and Repeatable Results,"[4]—I introduced readers to the three phases necessary to overcome challenges. The Stop, Step Back, and Grow cycle allows analytical as well as creative people to feel productive and comfortable with strategic goal setting. The next few pages introduce you to this remarkable organizational process that promotes a clear vision of your assets and guides you in building an intuitive and logical sequence of actions. What is the purpose of these steps? Fine-tuning your strategy for a successful future.

Stop!

In today's society, we have been programmed to keep running, keep making, keep selling, keep pushing. Go-go-go! No matter what, we're told to keep moving and we're seemingly brainwashed to perpetuate this exhausting lifestyle. If you are one of these do-do-do people, it may seem to you as though "stop" has become a nasty four-letter word.

Au contraire … **STOP!**

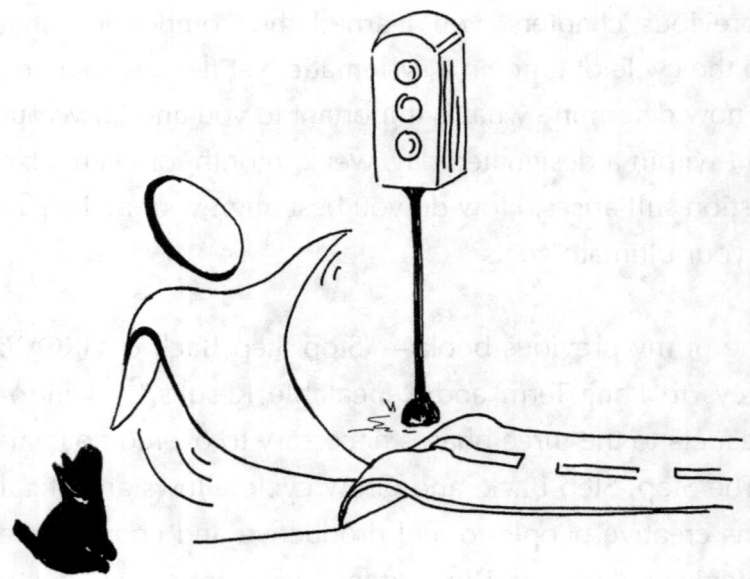

There is immeasurable value in using this simple freeze-stay reprieve regularly, both mentally and physically, and for the overall health of an organization or household. This single step is ultimately responsible for you being able to actualize your dreams. This Stop Phase empowers the mind (and any organization) to take note of the assets at hand now in order to put them to effective use later.

Imagine walking into a restaurant. The first thing the server brings you is a menu. This is an itemization of every dish and beverage they offer: appetizers, entrees, specialties, desserts, and à la carte items. Apply this same concept as it pertains to your life and career to create a menu of *you*. Your menu is an "inventory" of what you have.

Most of us feel like we are under a constant barrage of "a lot!" going on, so let's streamline. Position this initial Stop Phase of yourself as an affirmation, appreciation, or gratitude of haves, resources, and opportunities already accessible to you. You may start with your family, friends, personal possessions. Now I invite you to expand the concept to include what you know and who you know. Who knows you? What projects have you completed or what do you still want to achieve? This is *your* Stop Phase. Think big. Deem nothing as insignificant or irrelevant.

As you gather this remarkable registry of your assets (inventory), look for correlations or similarities. Discover parallels or connections among the items you included so that you can begin to group them. For example, from your list, what could you categorize as:

- Personal
- Career/Company
- Education/Special Skills/Certification
- Special People, Mentors, and Networks
- Service Items
- Retail Items
- Equipment/Property

Expand the list as you feel appropriate to your industry, business model, personal life, and other conditions surrounding you.

There is no wrong or right in this process. Any correlations you see between your assets are valid. Be assured, you will get to sort through all this soon.

Stopping is about recognizing where you are now and relearning and reacquainting yourself with what you have in your arsenal of resources. The emphasis is: What do you have *now*? Stopping is about assimilating the components around you and recognizing their context and value to progress within your family, career, or company.

Give yourself this space. Allow your muscles to relax; let your emotions rest. Permit your spirit and brain to take a breather. Yes, give your work a break. You read that right and, in this case, "work" may mean your job, studies, errands, social life—anything! I repeat: *Give your work a break.*

It is okay to pause and, for this moment, set other tasks aside. Realize that this concept is not about putting your entire business or life on hold, but rather about reallocating essential priorities as the foundation to a bigger future.

Consider retail stores. Every month, quarter, or for smaller businesses, at the very least every year, they conduct an inventory assessment. Taking inventory is anticipated and scheduled. During this time, employees are often freed from their regular roles to reallocate their time to account for the goods on hand. The inventory team leaves what they normally do and runs the count. Sometimes the store performs the audit after-hours or the store may even close its doors during this period. This Stop Phase applies the same concept to connect you with the resources you have available to you.

Before we go any further, I'd like you to appreciate the difference between stopping and quitting. Stopping is not the same as quitting. Quitting actively bars the future. Quitting entails actions (either conscious or subconscious) that prohibit you from continuing on that path again. In contrast, "stopping" is merely a pause in the journey that allows you to look around for safety, to refuel, to realign, or to hibernate until the time is right to start again. Stopping allows you to rest. Stopping also allows you to go. Turn your red light to green and you get to launch in any direction and with any speed that suits the circumstances and abilities you have at that time.

You have permission to *Stop*!

6 Time Plot 6: Stop!

List your inventory (wins, resources, skills, special clients, special employees, vendors, mentors, and any other assets you value):

_____

_____

_____

_____

Step Back

Attention all: Step Back!

"What?" you may ask incredulously. "What? First, I'm supposed to Stop and now I'm being asked to go backward?!"

It is not as counterintuitive as it may seem. Begin with a quick review of the Time Plot 3a and 3b (pp. 16-17) in chapter one in which you outlined and ranked your goals with the corresponding actions needed to achieve them. Appreciate that the clearer you establish your Wants, the easier it becomes for you to develop your plan. In these next few pages, you get to align all "the good stuff" that you just gathered in the previous section's Stop Phase (Time Plot 6, p. 54). This means it's time to assemble all applicable resources into a dynamic and productive order. This phase is the core of your strategy to success—one that is manageable, powerful, and geared to bring you closer to achieving your intended goal(s).

Envision a jigsaw puzzle in disarray on a tabletop. You search the scattered pile of pieces for the one that's distinctly half-green and half-purple. Assuming there is only one of these, it should be easy to find—right? But what if your eyes are just a few inches away from the surface where you can only see two or three pieces at a time? It's like being plopped in the middle of a random New York City intersection, looking for an ice cream shop you happened to see somewhere miles and hours before. Your search will inevitably take much, *much* longer—if you even locate what you're looking for before giving up. Now back away and picture the whole collection at once. There it is! You find that unique two-toned piece in a flash. *Snap!* It fits perfectly into the one spot where it belongs. By stepping back, you activated your discovery mode and added another solution to your own puzzle. It's the address to the ice cream store with a GPS to lead you right to it. You are another step closer to your vision.

Such is the advantage when you view your assortment of treasures and resources from a distance. Your strategy is to select pieces of your past and present to apply them in a dynamic and productive order. In other words, assemble your own jigsaw solution. Stepping Back opens up new perspectives so that you can now go shopping in your personal store of connections, skills, products, friends, lessons, etc.!

But just filling your shopping cart without a productive plan for implementation can quickly sabotage your efforts. It can become quite costly and is guaranteed to relentlessly zap your energy as you travel blindly without direction. At this time, I feel it's important to differentiate between a Plan of *Action* and what I call a Plan of *Progress*.

Let us bring the 2020 Lamborghini Aventador S into the discussion. At the time, this sports car was one of the most powerful cars in the world. One tap of the gas pedal hurtles its 730-horsepower, V12 engine from zero to 60 mph in 2.6 seconds! That is a *lot* of power. What does this have to do with planning for success? Supercars are designed for a dry, safe course. What happens when this powerful automobile encounters a snowstorm? The roads are slick, and the car slides off into a snowbank. Even when the driver pushes the pedal to over 5,000 rpm and the wheels spin faster, faster, and faster, the car doesn't budge an inch. In fact, the more the motor accelerates, the deeper the tires sink into the slick snow and ice and the less likely this beautiful machine will go anywhere. Action? Absolutely! Each of the ever-so-finely-tuned pistons is pounding at unimaginable speeds; the engine is roaring. Progress? None. Zilch. Our action-packed, luxurious race car remains motionless.

How many times have you felt like this machine? You are working eighteen-hours for six and even seven days a week to make everyone happy. You barely sleep. Yet, despite all your efforts, you feel stuck—you just can't seem to get anywhere. Without the application of a *viable* plan, we all can end up hopelessly spinning our wheels and, invariably, run the risk of burning out our own engines.

The Plan of *Progress* lets you access what you have, when you need it, to ultimately get what you want. It is a carefully planned acceleration to avoid the perilous spinout. It is the deliberate placing of sand and planks under your tires to give you the traction you need. It is the hitch you call upon to pull you safely out and onward.

The Stop Phase allows you to reacquaint yourself with your menu of *you*. Stepping Back is giving yourself the time in advance to assemble the relevant factors you have—with logic and an implementable strategy. Let creativity evolve and provide you with options, alternatives, and ultimately, solutions. This is why it is so important to Step Back and visualize the big picture. You want to be sure your steps make sense. Perhaps even more importantly, you must assure that every task you design is accessible and manageable. Hence, bringing you progress.

All the while, you choose the order that creates the most direct and easiest path to the goal and beyond! I have found that by ignoring this type of organized preplanning, too many well-intentioned people misuse assets or don't have them ready when they need them. Perhaps worst of all, they face some of their biggest challenges alone, completely overlooking who could have helped them. They miss the treasures hidden so close to them. Have you ever had that feeling? It's like inadvertently leaving your wallet at home and only remembering the twenty-dollar bills stashed in a back pocket after your friend had to pay for you. Poor planning is forgetting you have a cell phone to call a tow truck when you are stuck in a snowbank.

Or bolting awake in the middle of the night, thinking, "Why didn't I think of that before I just blew this opportunity?"

Where are you now, where are you going, and how are you getting there? The answers to these questions are crucial in transforming the Wants and Needs of your futuristic "I Will" into the active "I Am" of your excitingly progressive *now*.

This is where you ensure that each task (I Need to …) is realistic and achievable. As we reviewed before, if the task seems too daunting, then break it down to a new Want to be fulfilled by another set of smaller Need-to's. Anticipate that some Step Back's may take several weeks or longer, while others slip into place in a quick thirty-minute breakthrough. Pare it down to bite-size steps that meet your comfort level. Finally, rank the importance of each step in an order that allows you flexibility in the future.

So, *Step Back* and prepare to put your best foot forward!

7 Time Plot 7: Stepping Back

Reflect back to your goal from the first chapter's Time Plot 1. Step Back to review the resources you listed in the Time Plot 6: Stop! on Page 54. Create a list of steps that, when taken one after the other in an achievable order, will create a viable path to your goal:

My Plan of Progress:

First I will _____,
(Actionable Step)

then I will _____,
(Actionable Step)

and then I will _____.
(Actionable Step)*

This is your Plan of Progress!

*add as many actionable steps as you Need.

Grow

We arrive at the third action step: Grow! With this last phase of forming successful strategies, you progress from the planning stage into forward-moving action. You started with a dream, built it into a viable plan. Next, you LAUNCH! You are now making the journey real!

Preparation is simply the act of placing the *what* and *whom* you need ("I Can"), to *where* you need it, for *when* you need it ("I Will"). With the map clearly laid out at this point, there is nothing left to prevent you from activating your Plan of Progress ("I Am").

Yet why do so many of us still resist pulling the trigger? Consulting with business owners and company teams, I regularly see that it is the fear of, or the opposition to, change that is a very real barrier.

Many times I have worked with organizations facing change management and it quickly becomes evident that much of their struggle is a result of operations that have been passed down through countless generations of employees. One person would learn a process one way, show another, who, in turn, tweaks the technique with individual preferences, and then teaches the next. Why has the family pot roast always been trimmed into a rectangle for generations? Good meat was wasted for decades until someone finally realized that it had nothing to do with the actual recipe. Great-Great-Grandma had only cut the roast smaller so it would fit into a little pan—the only one she had.

Almost on cue, when I ask a team why they handle a process a certain way, I am faced with blank, sheepish stares, because no one has any idea. The characteristic response is, "Because that's how it's always been done."

Change is hard. Starting something new brings us into unfamiliar territory. It is this very unfamiliarity that instinctively invokes fear or at least caution. And here lies the challenging element to the best of intentions, one that can be astoundingly powerful in slowing us down, even paralyzing us into letting our dreams slip away.

You may be asking yourself why I am bringing up resistance to change now as we are talking about launches and growth. All too often, whether from a rebellious employee or simply the fear of the "new," defiance generally comes from the unknown. Resistance to change produces the strongest barriers to take-off mode. The good news is that it can also be one of the most preventable obstacles to overcome. Progress is within reach.

Dr. Stephen Porges, PhD, of the Kinsey Institute, has done extensive research on fear and phobias, providing physiological insight into our responses to safety and danger. We gravitate toward security and well-being. As he assesses responses to threatening situations, Dr. Porges finds that we have two distinctly different reactions: mobilization (fight or flight) or immobilization (shutting down or playing dead).[9]

Granted, facing a new strategy, a new technique, a new lifestyle, a new _____ *(I will let you, as the reader, fill in this blank)* may not compare fairly to an encounter with a hungry lion. But hopefully, you can see where the paradigm is going: We inherently fear change. These ensuing physiological reactions produce (1) a classic rejection of reform in favor of the status quo (immobilization) or (2) dodging the issue at hand entirely (flight). As a result, fear alone stands in the way of progress and the intended goal carries with it a remarkably high rate of failure.

The solution? Focus on strengthening your approach—the *fight* response! Mitigate the unknown with clear to-dos and expectations. Spell out the pathway and the means outlined in the Step Back phase for easy overview. By having your action steps chunked down so they are each ready and *viable* before you start, you dramatically reduce and even eliminate fear. In fact, comfort will replace anxiety and the clear preparations will invite you (your team) *toward* the safety of your plan!

Reviewing and being familiar with the discoveries during the Step Back phase creates the environment to best support your success. Remember, you approved these steps in your strategic Plan of Progress because you believed, perhaps even proved, they are actionable items. In other words, "Yes! You can!"

To further assure that you will advance, surround yourself with a likeness of what you want or where you want to be. Envision it. Taste it. Smell it. Hear it. Create an environment that envelopes you with people, programs, physical items, and anything you may need to support you in your launch. Experience it now through your senses as much as possible to prepare yourself to live it later.

Be clear of your vision. In business, we refer to visions as benchmarks. After all, how will you know when you achieve your goal if you can't identify your vision when you see it? Twenty percent growth in sales. Increase ratings by two points. Two new products in the next six months. Go camping at least once next summer. As accurately as possible, create *measurable* ways to define your successes. Translate "going out more" to "two date nights a month." Narrow down "eat better" more specifically to "one green vegetable with each meal."

By following these steps, when launch time arrives, you will find that your fears recede and that you're ready to follow through. "I Can" and "I Will" ease into "I Am" until it is *done*!

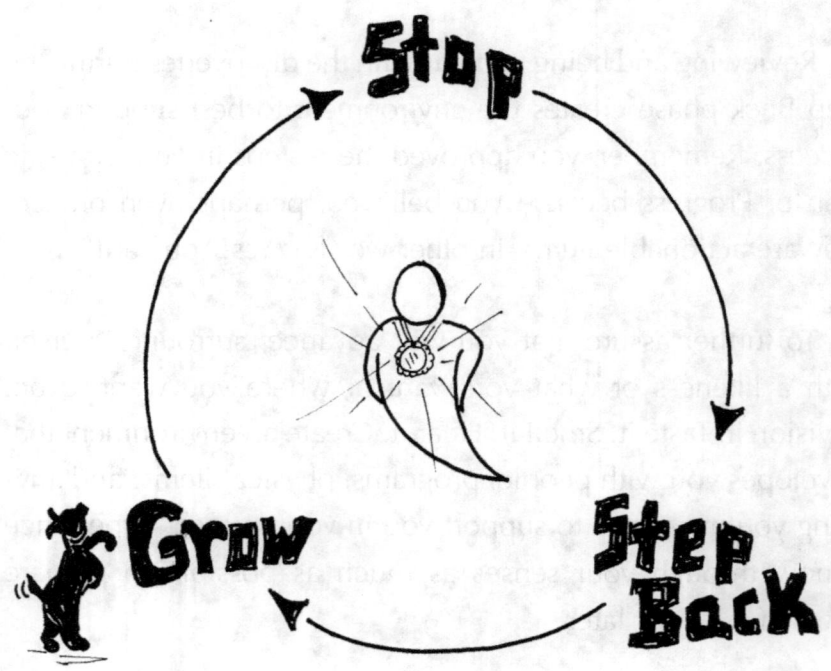

In contrast to being a "three-step program," the reality is that as you are continually bringing it all together. Stop, Step Back, and Grow is a self-sustaining, ever-flowing cycle. You reach your goal and you get to dream again. Stop! How wonderful is this? What's next? How can you most appreciate the success that *you* just achieved? Step Back and give yourself the gift of an unbiased overview only to grow, grow, GROW again!

Congratulations! After the following Time Plot, we tackle what so many want to know: How to stay accountable and how to effectively manage time.

8 Time Plot 8: GROW

What is your intended goal? _____

How will you know that you have reached your goal? List at least three of the action steps that got you closer to or helped you achieve this goal:

❏ 1.
❏ 2.
❏ 3.

Note the check boxes before each step. Celebrate your success by physically checking off what you have accomplished!

❏ Your final result: _____

CHAPTER 5

Beat the Clock, Part Two: Transferable vs. Timely

There are two main elements in developing an effective and easily accountable time management system. Both rely on the premise that our twenty-four hours are divided into multiple movable blocks of time as seen in chapter three. Each block is defined by unique meanings, varying sizes, and a variety of rigidity. To stay within the parameters of the determined container, if we want to adjust the *number* of blocks we must modify their sizes. Conversely, when the *size* of even a single block changes, we have to accommodate by increasing or decreasing the proportions of the other units, the quantity remaining, or both.

We start with Tier-One Time Management: Transferable Blocks and Timely Blocks. As we have established, each of these blocks represents a task, an appointment, or any other commitment you have in your day. Again, imagine the blocks as physical units that you can pick up and move into the context of a calendar.

A Transferable Block is a period of time that can be shifted from one location in your schedule to another without affecting the outcome. The Timely Block, on the other hand, demands concrete delegation to a particular date and time in your calendar and cannot be moved. How solidly each block must adhere to your allocated time slot depends entirely on the value you designate to it. Yes, the rigidity is ultimately your choice. See how it is all coming together?

Let's look at some examples as they apply to real life. Go back to chapter one's scenario in which you have worked so hard to secure the meeting with the CEO. We can assume that to close the deal there is no way you can move this appointment. After all, it took you three years to get this far, and the risks of moving it would likely irrevocably damage your credibility and the future outcome. The engagement that is slotted for Friday at 10 a.m. is Timely. Regard it set in stone.

The wedding with lots of people, weeks of planning for the perfect event: Timely. If, for whatever reason, "something comes up," you cannot move the date of the celebration. You just would not be going. Period.

On the other hand, your best friends have just moved back into town and you want to meet with them sometime in the next few weeks. They've already told you that they are delighted to see you whenever you can make it. You all decide on next Sunday for dinner. Then you get a last-minute invitation to the final baseball game of the season—but it's for that same Sunday night. The weather will be perfect, your whole softball league is going. Do you forego the game? Do you cancel the get-together with your best friends? You may not have to miss either. You call your friends. They are excited for you and reschedule your visit for Saturday (or maybe even Monday) and you allocate the time slot on Sunday for the big game. Perhaps you even invite them to go with you. All is good; you get to enjoy both activities because you simply (and respectfully) *transferred* the blocks to appropriately fit your needs.

An important aspect of Time Mapping is giving yourself permission to anchor and move your blocks based on the *value-choice-belief* system discussed earlier in chapter two.

To create the easily adhered-to Time Map schedule, first allocate the time blocks that you cannot move. Staff meetings or a networking event every third Thursday at 9 a.m.; family dinner nightly at 6:30 p.m.; softball practice Tuesdays and Thursdays at 5 p.m. Include personal time for yourself. Perhaps you set aside thirty minutes every morning at 7 a.m. to journal, work out, or _____ *(your choice)*. These are just examples. You know what your own obligations are.

As you organize your remaining tasks and obligations into additional blocks, you now build *around* what you have chosen as Timely zones. Once again, you will find it easier to sort these tasks. How "timely" they become is entirely based on their value to you.

While some commitments recur regularly, others may be one-offs, such as a doctor's appointment on a Wednesday or your father flying in March 20 for a three-day visit. You must actively reserve such events as rigid blocks in your calendar. Regardless of other personal, career, or school events, you set the doctor and Dad as top priorities, that is, as Timely obligations. They are rock-solid appointments in *your* world of commitments. These remain as scheduled, without an option to modify.

Keep in mind that any cancellations create a new time slot opening, and your twenty-four-hour calendar then has another empty spot to fill. Relax! The intention is not to pack your day into a busy hustle from morning until night. Rather, you now have an even greater choice. Leave the recent opening blank to accommodate last-minute hiccups, or slip in a new task you thought you didn't have time for previously. Or, and this is where life gets beautiful: Just set yourself free and block the empty spot for some quiet time and self-care!

As you become more comfortable with this jigsaw puzzle approach to your calendar, you will gain a better oversight of your schedule as well as increased flexibility. Experiment! You can now customize which task, obligation, or desire you wish to add or delete based on the value you allocate to each. Play around with switching one or two of your Transferable Blocks if that fits better.

A word of caution: Before you hastily transfer new appointments or tasks back and forth, double-check why you scheduled the initial event where you had it in the first place. Just because it is Transferable, does not mean that you didn't have a good reason for putting it there to start. Was traffic a factor for your original timing? Did you need to get X done before Y? Did weather play a part in it? I have made plenty-a-mess for myself changing things around, realizing too late that, because of the adjustments, I wasted an hour traveling to meet people at different times of the day at the same place. The reality is, you control your power over time as you relocate blocks based on where they fit best. The concept of transferability permits you to move things accordingly with the bonus of not letting them drop off your schedule and fade away, forgotten.

Indeed, there will be times when even a Timely Block must be rearranged. Your car breaks down. Your CEO will be in town *only* when you normally work out. I strongly suggest, however, that if you find yourself moving a lot of Timely appointments, (1) reassess what you consider "commitments" and (2) verify that you are still respecting your own time.

Remember to include work and personal blocks. Fit in your projects, errands, chores. Include your Need-to's and Wants. Respect your commitment to this plan. It is *your* plan. Own it! By understanding your obligations to your time slots and the consequences for moving (or *not* moving) them, you will find your schedule becoming much easier to follow.

9 Time Plot 9:
Tier-One Time Management: Transferable vs. Timely

The calendar schematics you completed on pages 44-47 at the end of chapter three will help you build your new Time Mapping schedule. Apply this Time Plot as an open, creative canvas waiting for you to fashion your schedule according to your lifestyle.

In the next three months or more of your own calendar*:

1. List all your regularly scheduled (Timely) commitments.

2. Add all special occasions, events, tasks you know in the time(s) you expect them or would like them to be. (These may be Timely or Transferable.)

3. Insert blocks for you-time, hobby-time, family-time, project-time, house-time. This list is an open, creative canvas waiting for you to fashion according to your lifestyle. (These may also be Timely or Transferable.)

4. In any manner that feels and looks right to you, mark the Timely start times. Examples: Highlight, circle, digitally locking

*Calendar choices will be addressed in chapter seven.

CHAPTER 6

Beat the Clock, Part Three: Fixed vs. Flexible

Tier Two in Time Mapping lends itself to the size of the time blocks you create. You have assigned Timely or Transferable to trigger when to start a particular activity, but *how long* should each last? When do you end the coffee meeting arranged to "get to know each other?" At what point do you cut the drafting process short and hit the send button?

To stay on track, we must set parameters. For example, how often have we fit in a quick lunch with someone, and before we knew it, two hours had flown by? We finally get back to the office, only to find ourselves massively behind on emails that would have promised a much higher return for the time invested.

Does "I have no idea where my time went!" sound familiar as you struggle to complete the errands you had set out to do that very morning?

By preassigning the beginning *and* the end, like gatekeepers, we avoid these open-ended time-suckers. We can also allow ourselves the guilt-free pleasure of "however long it takes" when we plan for it accordingly.

Recall that time blocks are each assigned to one activity. Remember, too, that all the blocks we establish in our schedule must still fit within the twenty-four-hour day just like all the blocks have to fit inside the toy box I described. Regardless of tagging it as a Timely or Transferable Block, you can either make it Fixed with a preset period (one hour, thirty minutes, four days) or Flexible by allowing expansion or shrinking of the block size. Think of an accordion stretching to fill with air and collapsing as it gets squeezed back together.

But, reality check, we know everything still must fit into the lovely twenty-four hour box. All the tasking/appointment blocks have to align within the framework of your schedule. If you expand one period of time in your calendar, then per the law of physics, you must reduce the size of another. Or you need to take one item out of that day or week's schedule and transfer it to another block where it will fit.

A blind date is a perfect example of this. The couple begins with a cordial coffee meeting at 3 p.m. Within a few minutes, at least one person has usually decided how they feel about the other. Let's pretend it's not going so well. Does the hapless duo continue to chat about meaningless trivia for the next one or two hours? Or does one of them recognize the futility of the meeting, and within thirty minutes thank the other for coming and then politely leave? The latter saves time, likely money, and even potential heartache in the long run.

And we can appreciate the romantic flipside of the story: The two hit it off so well that their coffee date continues long into the evening. Both are certain they have just met their soul mate. Business meetings should be treated similarly. I have courteously cut phone calls short once it became clear the call was purely a sales pitch for something I had no interest in. Conversely, with other meetings, you may intentionally choose to spend more time that could produce meaningful partnerships with people and companies that you'll still do business with years later.

In the previous stories' outcomes, the length of the "date" is modified to fit the needs and value of the activity itself. The application of Fixed and Flexible time slots provides an accountable structure while allowing for accommodations to an ever-changing day. I am quick to establish the value of my precious time and usually have little trouble establishing my "Yes" or "No." You can too.

The key word here is "accountable." Plan accordingly. Always include some flexibility to help provide a buffer when things don't go as planned. It is important to be aware that if you choose to Flex with an option to lengthen the time frame of an activity in your schedule, do not schedule a Timely appointment afterward without an appropriate buffer zone. Also, prepare in advance what you can and *will* do with any time gained if the task gets done earlier than anticipated: Do you move one of your other Transferable Blocks into this vacant seat? Do you redirect this bonus time to something new that you thought you could not do before? Keep in mind that free time (or, as I like to call it, *Me* Time) is perfectly acceptable and even strongly encouraged. Again, if you are aware of the allocation and it is appropriately applied, then by all means take advantage of more self-care whenever you can!

Of course, this is where it gets tricky. How much flexibility do we allow? How stringently do we enforce a specific time slot? An extension of Parkinson's law implies that if we have a longer stretch of time to complete a task, we will likely use the entire allotment. In contrast, we may complete the same project in a much shorter time if that's all we have.[5] Our ability to finish a task is directly related to the amount of time we are allowed to complete it. Sometimes we must create boundaries for ourselves so that we don't expend more time resources on a task that could have been completed much faster. Get it done!

Let's review the *value-choice-belief* standings and reapply them here. When we maintain a big overview picture and consciously acknowledge and accept the outcome of our actions, then for the most part we can trust what we do. It is the responsible application of what you value most feeding into these choices you make. Big picture!

Fixed periods keep you on track. Flexible slots allow you to maximize the effectiveness of or creativity in each moment to your constantly changing needs and desires. Remember to include cushions throughout your schedule to accommodate for the Flex times you build into your day. Determine in advance what in your schedule must remain Fixed versus Flexible to hold you accountable and keep you on track. Once you embrace and integrate this component of Time Mapping, you will find that staying on course vastly reduces your stress and encourages a guilt-free schedule.

10 Time Plot 10:
Tier-Two Time Management: Fixed vs. Flexible

Return to your calendar. In the gaps of your calendar, identify where you can assign Fixed Blocks to focus your efforts. Take into consideration travel time, preparation, etc.

Evaluate where your Flexible Blocks may be and how you will maximize the value received with this "open" time.

CHAPTER 7

Building the Legend: Your Master Map to Success

We finally step into drawing your Master Time Map! With each "I Will" transforming into "I Am" all the concepts you have learned can now be gathered into one functional Time Map or, as may sound more familiar to you, your calendar. The stronger you embrace your Time Map, the more your stress levels will significantly (if not entirely) drop. Your lifestyle becomes productive and relaxed at the same time. Staying on track becomes simplified and easy to maintain.

First, which is best as your primary mapping medium: virtual or paper?

In our highly digitized world, many of us have adopted at least some level of online scheduling. Calendars sync, appointments auto-populate, reminders and notifications ping us exactly as we have programmed them to do. Though the convenience of this wide-ranging system allows us to have full access from wherever we may be, I have found that relying purely on a digital calendar jeopardizes the ten-thousand-foot overview that is so important to foster our ultimate satisfaction.

For those who choose to stick to online schedulers, I do advocate for finding an all-in-one source or an integration app that allows you to retrieve the multiple functions you need at once. By using multiple platforms for various tasks, invites, client databases, appointments, memberships, personal events, etc., you are losing precious time signing in and out of each as well as potentially increasing subscription fees. You also dramatically increase the risk of inadvertently overlapping your time blocks when accessing nonintegrating systems. Perhaps even most importantly, you can quickly lose sight of your goals. The result? Wasted time, more mistakes, increased frustration, higher stress, and tragically too often, lost dreams.

I strongly encourage anyone wishing to implement the highest level of time management to embrace paper planners. Even if you continue to access online schedulers, adding a hard copy organizer offers powerful benefits. Using both can work well, as long as you consciously apply the tools, knowing the appropriate purpose and intended result of each.

Before I developed the physical Time Map Organizer[6] in 2014, I was frustrated because I couldn't find one scheduling system that fit all my Needs. (I say "Needs" here because without the systems in place, I knew I could not reach my Wants.) I Wanted a detailed hourly, daily, weekly, *and* monthly overview, all visible in one glance. I Wanted to be able to easily set my goals and have them in front of me as a constant reminder and incentive. I Wanted the freedom to add notes and move things around, without having to repeatedly rewrite and reorganize. So I designed the Time Map Organizer, which I still use nearly a decade later. I am not alone. Although countless new apps and online scheduling platforms are still being produced, I continue to hear of more and more people returning to paper calendars.

Here is why physical Time Mapping works. Research repeatedly proves the powerful impact on our brain and mindset through the simple tangible application of pen to paper. In 2020, the Norwegian University of Science and Technology's Department of Psychology released an analysis of education in children and young adults. Researchers studied how typewritten versus handwritten materials affected learning. The results showed significant improvement in memory retention when the students wrote their notes by hand.[7] How does this fit in with our calendars? By capturing thoughts (tasks, goals, inspirations) in a handwritten format, we further imprint purpose, actions, and intentions into our brain.

I find that people who struggle with time management also have frustrations with accountability. The focus must be on mindset. Accountability relies on commitment, and commitment is the foundation of follow-through. How can we further support our convictions and embed our accountability with a particular action? There is a palpable realness we experience by writing down our thoughts and by manually crossing out our to-dos as they get completed. (Recall the celebration by checking off your successes in your p. 68 Time Plot 8: Grow.)

A frequently referenced study published by Mueller and Oppenheimer, researchers of psychology, demonstrates additional benefits of longhand writing. In contrast to using a keyboard, when we apply pen to paper, our brain processes content far more effectively.[8] Handwriting subliminally forces us to sift through information in greater detail. It gives us time to analyze and question the topic at hand. Is this feasible? Is this what I want to or can do? Our neurons fire through a complex series of their own strategies to assess fact or fiction and adds the action to memory. Accountability thus becomes further ingrained into our conscious and subconscious habits.

Regardless of whether you use a paper or digital calendar, it is also critical to recognize the importance of maintaining oversight. Think back to the Stop Phase of chapter four: What is happening in your scheduling, opportunities, and current lifestyle? Cross-reference your day with your week into your year and beyond. Examine the patterns of your schedule as it pertains to your ultimate goals. By doing so, you have now empowered yourself to stay organized and on course. Granted, digital notifications can remind us of appointments in real time. But consider a yellow highlighted note or a red-inked appointment in a paper organizer right in front of you. These visuals may be more difficult to overlook in comparison to an electronic alarm you can easily snooze or dismiss.

Many would agree that we possess inner timing signals that somehow send us mindful prompts. Nowadays, however, most of us have relinquished the majority of these formerly natural cues to fully robotic notifications. Automated reminders have evolved far beyond the exciting "You've got mail" to a constant barrage of "bings" announcing texts, meetings, bills, holidays, vacations, and even trash days. The list goes on and on *and on* as we dumb ourselves down with our ever-increasing reliance on our devices. How many errands, phone numbers, or birthdays can we recall without the token bells or stored memory apps? Unused muscles atrophy and grow weak. Our brain is no different.

Another critical challenge we must address is the constant impingement of ever-expanding societal distractions. Digital-only or online scheduling can intrude on our ability to fully implement the focus that Time Mapping offers. For one, when the infamous little "bing" or song snippet sounds the alarm, our concentration and flow is instantly interrupted. All too frequently, this seems to happen at the most inopportune times. A conversation is cut short midsentence. The perfect words in the Pulitzer Prize–winning commentary we just had in our head are gone in a flash. How do we stay focused with interruptions pulling our attention in so many directions, often minutes or even seconds apart?

Let us also be aware of how reminders can lead to a dangerous charade in preparedness. Perhaps in the most simplified example, the soft "ping" notifies you of your working lunch with Casey at noon. But that is just when the meeting starts. What about the time needed to transition to the meeting? A quick check of emails before you head out, packing your laptop and newly printed flyers, touch-up of makeup, tie, directions, and traffic, etc.? These actions must be planned for. Realize, too, that this automated reminder was only for this next appointment. What about the visit with your significant other you had planned afterward? Did you remember to bring the cookies you baked last night for the two of you? Without the oversight of the whole day, we end up rushed, unprepared in mindset, inevitably forgetting something, or even being late to the very appointment for which we had set the reminder. Be sure you scan over your entire day every morning. Before the end of today, check your Time Map for tomorrow and the remaining week.

I alluded to it before: One major drawback from relying too much on digital reminder systems is that once you acknowledge the notification, it disappears. When you snooze it, once again you set yourself up for recurring interruptions. Also, how do you keep your big vision and goals actively in front of you in a sustainable and easily accessible manner?

My point is not to discount the admittedly efficient online or smart device logic. Rather, I want you to see gaps in which your physical organizer can help and how to maximize the benefits of digital and physical schedulers if you choose to use both. Have fun with this. Perhaps experiment with several calendars at the same time to find one that best suits all your needs. Make sure you use one that you can easily access. If you are interested to learn more about the Time Map All-in-One Organizer/Scheduler, please visit the reference section of this book. The trick is to control how you assemble your own jigsaw puzzle of time effectively. The main emphasis is about what do *you* want? Which system is right for you?

Most of us have already discovered that we can't really "manage" time. Time management is a fallacy. Instead, achieving success in our lives is about managing *ourselves*. Ultimately, the Gift of Time is to create a beautiful end-product image of the life you want. No matter which scheduling or planning format you choose, you want your Time Map to be your accompanying guide. Calendars act as reminders. Planners keep our goals in front of us, encourage our vision, and should naturally pull us toward our intended destination. Time Mapping brings everything together and keeps us on track.

This is the perfect moment to share the story of a philosophy professor who wants to demonstrate the value of time and effort to his class. He places an empty jar on his desk and pours in a handful of sand. Then he adds a collection of small pebbles, and finally tops it off with a few larger rocks. The contents are piled high above the rim, making closing the lid impossible.

He empties out the glass and starts anew. This time, however, he reverses the process. First, he drops the bigger stones into the jar. Then adds the pebbles, many of which slip between the crevices made by the rocks below. Lastly, the professor drops in the sand, most of which trickles around the pebbles and rocks in the jar. Lo and behold, this time everything fits and he pops on the lid with plenty of room to spare!

The story illustrates that when we start with the difficult tasks first (as exemplified by the large rocks) it opens up the needed room to add the easier tasks (smaller pebbles). To be clear, "big" can represent something that may be difficult or time-consuming to complete, such as developing a detailed annual report. Or it can mean a task that we just don't want to do, like cleaning the house or responding to a customer complaint.

Motivational books and talks around the world have used this story so much that the true origin has sadly long been lost. But I believe the professor's solution to filling the jar doesn't tell the whole story. While tackling the big challenges in our lives does help us move our mountains, in some ways this take-on-the-big-stuff strategy can be shortsighted and at times self-defeating.

How often have we fallen behind on the day-to-day responsibilities because we were "buried" by a big project we had to get done? *I have to finish the manuscript before I pay the bills. This proposal has to get out to the client and* then *we'll have our staff meeting. We need to finish painting the living room before we take a walk on this warm spring day.* When we focus too much of our time and efforts on large undertakings (the big rocks), too frequently we allow the "little" things to pass us by. *I'll send out that payment tomorrow… I'll exercise tomorrow… I'll reconnect with the team tomorrow… tomorrow … tomorrow.*

When we pressure ourselves to start with and focus on just those big rocks until they get done, it doesn't take long before it's the end of the day and we missed the chance for the little things, like calling a friend on their birthday. The bills still haven't been paid. Tomorrow becomes yesterday. Day has turned to night, Spring into Winter, and it's like the sand has slid through the hourglass instead into the jar of our time.

In the professor's demonstration, he adhered strictly to working from largest to smallest. His technique relies on the fate of trickle-down to fill the gaps. I suggest slightly adjusting his model. Indeed, we should start with a large job (a big rock). But as we continue to add to our jars, instead of following the large to small tactic, weigh in which of the various-sized tasks could fit best into the space available. By alternating the medium tasks (pebbles) *and* the smaller to-dos (sand) as they fit best, we create a custom design while avoiding bottle-necks caused by the huge projects that go on and on. In this manner, we cushion and seat the spaces far more effectively while loading the glass at our own, healthy pace.

Weave mini-blocks of easy tasks into your tough jobs. Choose a medium-sized, lower intensity project after a quick errand, before restarting the big chore. By alternating the longer, difficult tasks with faster, simpler to-dos, you will accomplish far more in a single day. This technique makes it painless to set aside a five minutes to send your birthday greetings, plan for breaks to walk around the block, or get groceries on the way home from work. Think of all the checkboxes you can cross off! You will also feel refreshed, hence much more efficient because your mind gets rest and your body experiences more variety too. Just be sure to commit to your scheduled blocks in order to stay accountable to all the tasks (big and small) as our professor suggested.

Finally! You now have all the tools you need to launch your journey. You have drawn a map leading you right to your goal(s), and just as importantly, pinpointing where you started. You defined and clarified which tasks needed completion for you to reach your Wants. You created an organizing system in which to log and track every Want and Need to get you to your goal.

Every day you may face a continuous bombardment of commitments: driving the kids to school, client emergencies, new refrigerator, going to work or school, customer complaints, sleep, mowing the lawn, a friend in need. The list goes on and on. Your key to keeping the flurry of dos, can-dos, and don't-dos under control is to recognize that you always have the ability to sort them based on what is most important at this time or for the future. It is just a matter of making conscientious decisions based on the values you set.

We have to *accept* that we get to choose to do whatever is most vital in our life. Going to work may not be the most fun choice, but we know we have to pay for our home and food, so we work. Seeing our son's or daughter's happy face on graduation day is a no-brainer, so we know we will be there—no matter what. The actions leading up to your desired results come down to *believing* facts, common sense, and your gut. The more often you consciously review your options and trust your decisions, the easier the habit becomes.

The plan is to assemble the many pieces of your days into increments that make sense for you. Perhaps you schedule fifteen minutes for travel time or a morning routine. Or you may delegate tasks in one-hour increments. I cannot stress this enough: Whatever works for *you*. I generally schedule in thirty-minute increments, adding intermittent fifteen-minute unassigned "sessions" to act as cushions for breaks, traffic, a quick phone call, or just a much-needed pause.

Start scheduling by opening your calendar. As outlined in the Timely vs. Transferable section in chapter five, this road map is your cornerstone. Pencil in (or key in if you are on a digital device) everything you can think of. Again, start with your Timely commitments (to others and yourself), then add Transferable ones as appropriate. As much as possible, create concrete guidelines for yourself in advance that address where you can modify or when to hold firm to your scheduled (committed) blocks.

I encourage color coding (different categories if you're using a digital calendar). Use a multicolored pen or a highlighter, each shade representing a different purpose, flexibility, or any other grouping essential to your own organization.

This is your journey. This is your Time Map.

11 Time Plot 11: Fine-Tune Your Time Map

- *Schedule your Timely events (work and personal).*
- *Specify the Fixed or Flexible amount of time allocated with each Timely period.*
- *Add in your Transferable events, evaluating how the scheduling of these activities can help you reduce travel and preparation time and increase focus and direction toward your ultimate desires.*
- *Specify the Fixed or Flexible amount of time allocated with each Transferable period.*

The world is constantly changing. If we stay where we are, our world will fly past us, and we will be left behind. Learn from others; embrace the new. Evolving and adapting with your Plan of Progress is the foundation to growth and success. We must adjust and rework ourselves to accommodate our current environment—even to stay a step ahead. Crafting our new Wants is what converts our intentions ("I Can," "I Will") to reality ("I Am").

Our goal is to overcome the detours and demons impeding our progress. Recognizing and confronting these challenges proactively can decrease our stressors and release the guilt we carry about not being able to accomplish everything. We can now transform obstacles into direction and new destinations. Activating our creativity and improving our functionality allows us to find and apply the resources we have. Our own motivations and strengths take us further than we ever imagined we could go.

Moving past our fears goes far beyond overcoming obstacles. Consider the realization made by Lucas LaFreniere and Michell Newman of the Pennsylvania State University Department of Psychology, who found that over 90 percent of our worries never happen.[10] I know that my journey will continue in the years to come, with the Time Map always at my side. I am excited for you too!

I encourage you to revisit your Want-o-Meter frequently! It can be a powerful reminder and motivator to your true self. Activate your goal setting, your visions, and your manifesting mindset. Be the controller of the viable strategy to map *your* journey to work-life balance, to growth, and to the fulfilling life you so deserve.

12 Time Plot 12:
Transforming Your Time Map into Your TreasureMap

Review your Wants. Review your schedule every morning and evening for your day, week, month, and beyond.

- *Are you scheduling what is important to you? Are your actions leading you, allowing you to live the life you choose?*
- *What are you willing to change to make your life even better?*
- *How is your schedule bringing you closer to your greatest desires?*
- *What can you modify, add, or remove to bring you the "now" you wish to have?*

You have told yourself, "I Can." You have even evolved past "I Will." Let go of the guilt. Your moment is about you, and you have every right to fill your cup before you tend to the rest of the world. You are a mover and a shaker! Shout it out there for everyone to hear: "I Am!"

Don't see time as your obstacle or enemy. On the contrary, time is your friend. Experience is the essence of "I Am." Experience is the success in living the life we choose. Traveling *with* time allows us to experience the world. From here on out, travel *with* time. Simply by being you, you have found the powerful Gift of Time. Receive it.

References

1. Georgia McIntyre, "What Percentage of Small Businesses Fail? (And Other Need-to-Know Stats)" *Fundera Data and Reports,* November 20, 2020, https://www.fundera.com/blog/what-percentage-of-small-businesses-fail.

2. Michael A. Lombardi, "Why Is a Minute Divided into 60 Seconds, an Hour into 60 Minutes, Yet There Are Only 24 Hours in a Day?" *Scientific American,* March 5, 2007, https://www.scientificamerican.com/article/experts-time-division-days-hours-minutes/.

3. Wolfgang Pauli, "Exclusion Principle and Quantum Mechanics, Nobel Lecture, December 13, 1946, https://www.nobelprize.org/uploads/2018/06/pauli-lecture.pdf.

4. Ingrid Pyka, DVM, Cert VMI, *Stop! Step Back and Grow: The Three Keys to Long-Term and Repeatable Success* (Highlands Ranch: TreeMark Publishing, 2018).

5. Wikipedia, "Parkinson's law," s.v., last modified October 23, 2021, 8:33, https://en.wikipedia.org/wiki/Parkinson%27s_law.

6. Ingrid Pyka, DVM, Cert VMI, *Time Map Calendar & Organizer* (Highlands Ranch: TreeMark Publishing, 2021).

7. Eva Ose Ashkvik, F. R. (Ruud) van der Weel and Audrey L H, van der Meer, "The Importance of Cursive Handwriting Over Typewriting for Learning in the Classroom: A High-Density EEG Study of 12-Year-Old Children and Young Adults," *Frontiers in Psychology* (July 28, 2020), https://www.frontiersin.org/articles/10.3389/fpsyg.2020.01810/full

8. Pam A. Mueller and Daniel M. Oppenheimer, "The Pen Is Mightier Than the Keyboard: Advantages of Longhand Over Laptop Note Taking," *Sage Journals* 25, no. 6 (April 2014): 1159–1168, https://journals.sagepub.com/doi/10.1177/0956797614524581

9. "The Polyvagal Theory for Treating Trauma," a teleseminar session with Stephen W. Porges, PhD, and Ruth Buczynski, PhD, The National Institute for the Clinical Application of Behavioral Medicine, https://static1.squarespace.com/static/5c1d025fb27e390a78569537/t/5cce03089b747a3598c57947/1557005065155/porges_nicabm_treating_trauma.pdf.

10. Lucas S. LaFreniere and Michelle G. Newman, "A Brief Ecological Momentary Intervention for Generalized Anxiety Disorder: A Randomized Controlled Trial of the Worry Outcome Journal," *Depression and Anxiety* 33(9), 829-839, May 15, 2019. https://papers.ssrn.com/sol3/papers.cfm?abstract_id=3383192

Acknowledgments

An incredible thank you to Jules Marie, my amazing, diligent, patient, detail-oriented, and always-so-sweet editor. (This run-on sentence alone would have put her over the edge!) Your continued support in the multiple manuscript renditions has been truly priceless. Another note of deep appreciation must also go to Bob Schram, who, endured my chronic "what if it looks this way...or that?" and managed to create this beautifully designed book.

Gary Barnes, as usual, your long friendship and wise insights are priceless. Thank you to my many beta-readers who invested your valuable time to support this project. Your feedback will always be indispensable and your support thoroughly appreciated.

I must also applaud my nephew, Martin Pyka. With his astounding graphic art talent, he managed to pull the visions out from my head for the conceptual designs carried throughout *I Can. I Will. I Am.* And, to Linda Pilgrim, my deepest gratitude for completing these wonderful illustrations. You have brought the jumpy-persona to life!

And, of course, to my two daughters, Krista and Maria—thank you for helping make me who I am!

I am proud and honored to have each of you on my team.

Get the complete Stop! Step Back & GROW here!

Your step-by-step solutions through problem-solving in one place.

Looking for an easy way to plan and track your progress?

Use this supplementary Blueprint to fully activate your success!

1ˢᵗ Place Award winner, Dr. Ingrid's easy goal-setting and goal-achieving program has been inspiring people around the world.

"Page after page of actionable tips and techniques…
to keep you moving!"
MARK HARDCASTLE, Airline Pilot

"This book and the knowledge you shared is liberating,
even life changing."
AMY COLLETTE, Author & Author Coach

"Not only does this book explain the process, but it provides the blueprint we need to execute our strategy and achieve our goals."
COURTNEY BERG, SHRM-SCP, SPHR

"Foundation for success!'
GARY BARNES, International Speaker and Traction Coach

Order yours now!
www.ingridpyka.com

Time Mapping©
Calendar & Planner

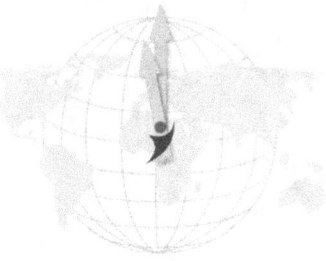

Ready to use the Time Map Organizer Planner?

Get started with your day, week, and month finally organized into ONE-VIEW!

Work-life balance at your finger-tips!

Balance your life–the way you've always wanted!
www.ingridpyka.com

About the Author

After providing medical care through private, corporate, general, specialty/ER animal hospitals, and even a housecall practice of her own, Dr. Ingrid Pyka realized helping companies and employees both thrive had become her true calling.

She received her doctorate from Colorado State University's Veterinary School and furthered her business certification at Purdue University. Ingrid quickly took on more administrative roles and her passion in management transformed into full-time consulting for veterinary practices, other small businesses and entrepreneurs. She now travels nationwide, training and speaking to audiences in and outside of the veterinary profession about effective systems and simplification. Her goal is to integrate maximum work-life balance with sustainable business practices.

Ingrid grew up in California, but has lived in Colorado for well over half of her life. She still "keeps her fingers furry" with occasional relief veterinary work. When not traveling or working, she enjoys gardening, ballroom dancing, and, just sitting out in nature—doing nothing.

What do you say?
We still want to see your insights!

Go here for to add your responses to
Dr. Ingrid's Time Survey:

www.ingramcontent.com/pod-product-compliance
Lightning Source LLC
Chambersburg PA
CBHW072039110526
44592CB00012B/1480